ECHO ENIGMA
An Exhibition by Scott Froschauer

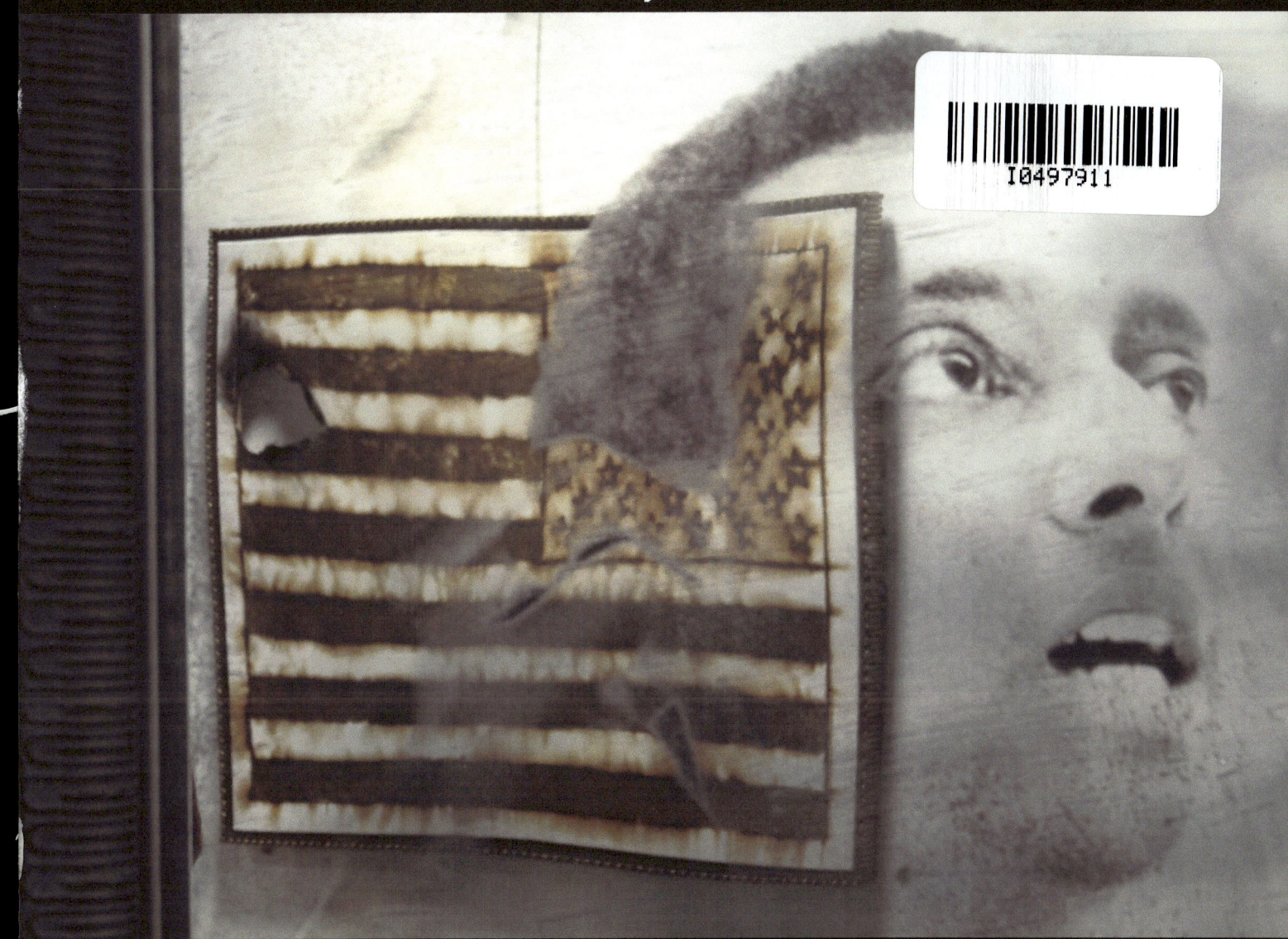

Curated by Kira Vollman

© 2018 Scott Froschauer-All Rights Reserved-ISBN 978-1719514026

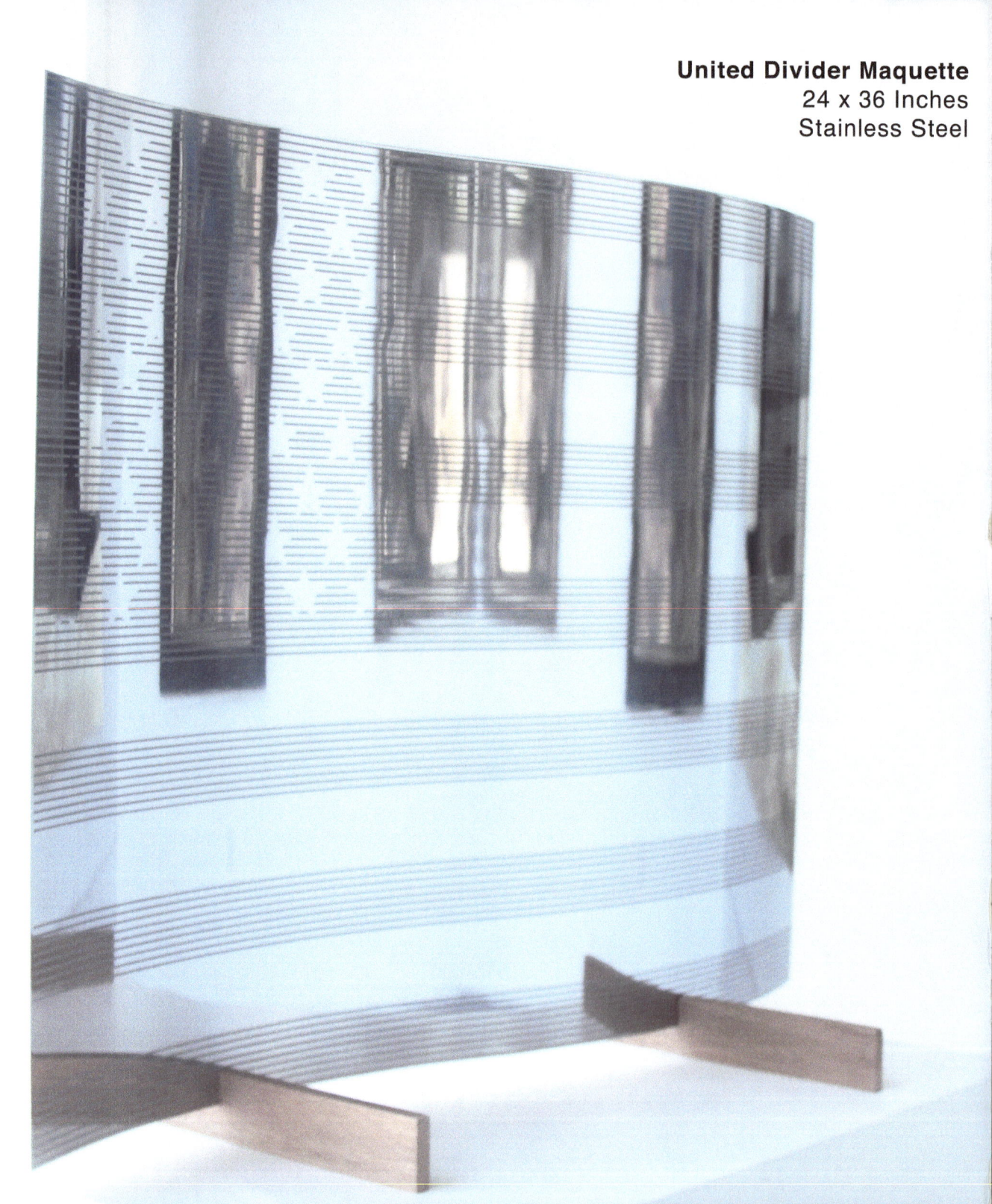

United Divider Maquette
24 x 36 Inches
Stainless Steel

The United Divider is a proposal for a large scale sculpture consisting of a 15' tall 20' wide plate of stainless steel, etched with the design of an American flag and curved to give the appearance of billowing in the wind. The engraving on the mirror polished surface of the sculpture consists of names of historic American figures.

The American Flag stands at a crossroads of belief systems and perspectives. "I am an American" is a statement that holds a great deal of shame and pride. Being American is a complex reality.

By representing the names of historic Americans as the fabric the American Flag is constructed of, United Divider seeks to explore the multi-faceted nature of America.

Each name that is engraved onto the piece is a hero to some and a villain to others.

Our national dialog drifts towards a greater degree of polarization, pushing the perspective on these individual names towards sainthood or demonization. This work seeks to witness their humanity.

The surface of the piece is mirrored to reflect those who gaze on it as America is merely a vessel for our beliefs. The characterization of the individuals engraved on it is derived from a particular viewer. The monumental scale of the finished piece is designed to create a separation, a divider, between those standing on each side of it.

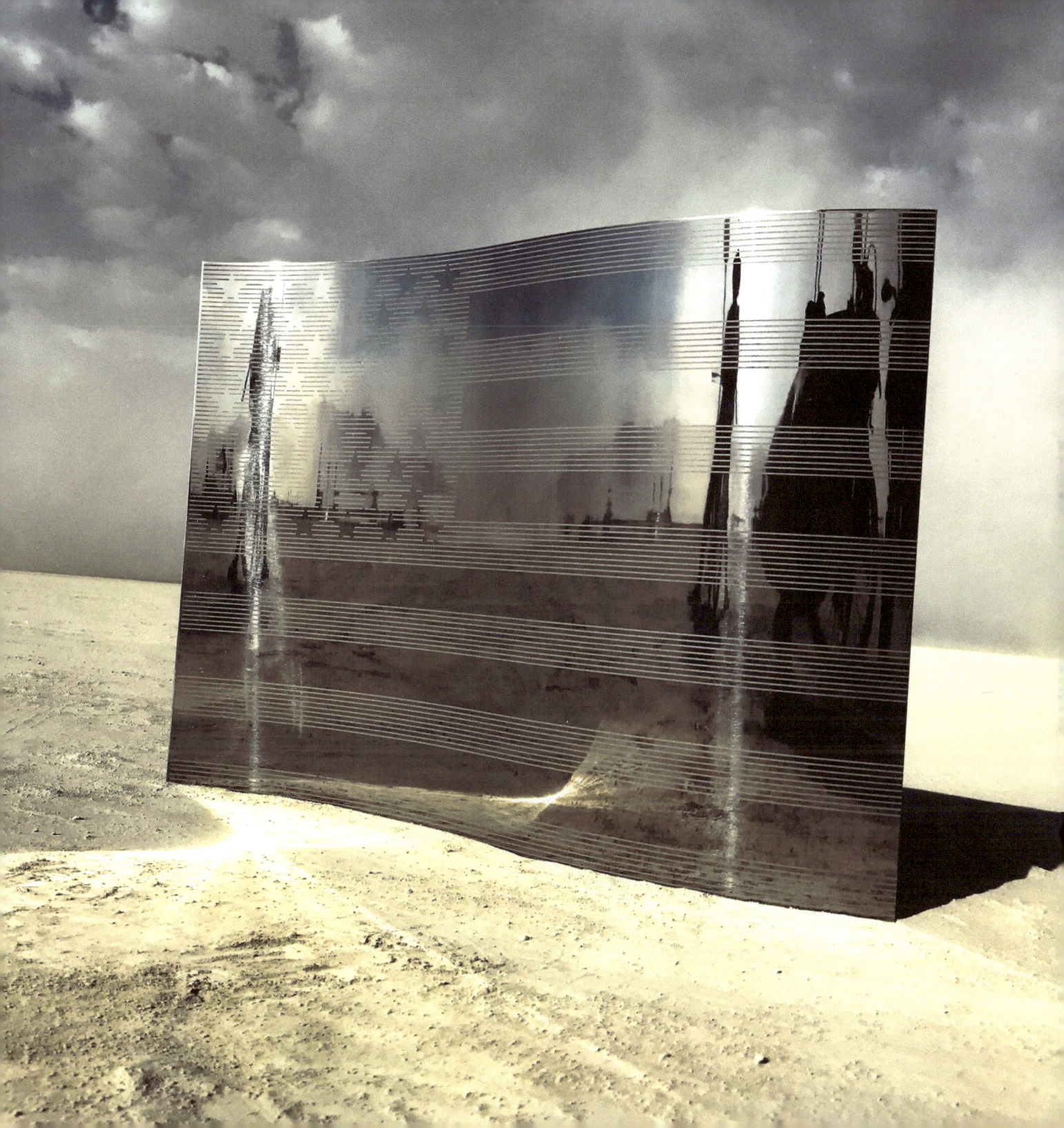

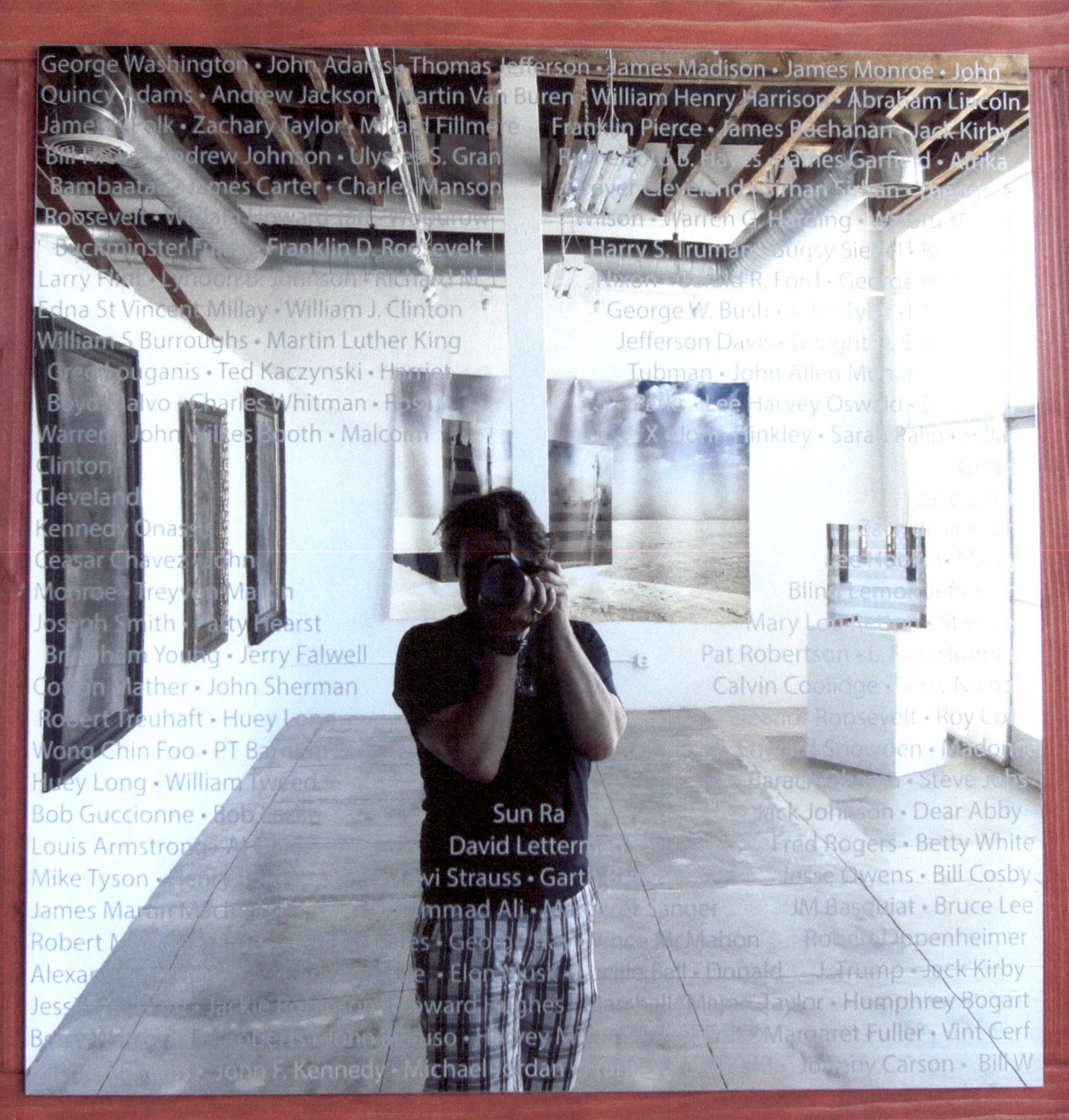

Pat Robertson • L. Ron Hub
Calvin Coolidge • Terry Ni
Eleanor Roosevelt • Roy
Edward Snowden • Ma
Barack Obama • Steve
Jack Johnson • Dear
Fred Rogers • Betty

Full Scale Detail of One Star from United Divider
Polished Stanless Steel
Sandblasted Text
Wood Frame

The Portraits

These portraits are studies of those who are named in the United Divider. Echo Enigma is the name of the technique used to present these studies. Each piece consists of an image imbedded in a distressed, hand poured mirror, as the stature of the portrayed subject is a reflection of the viewer.

These individuals embody a complexity that can be represented in a variety of ways depending on the brevity of the story and the perspective of the historian.

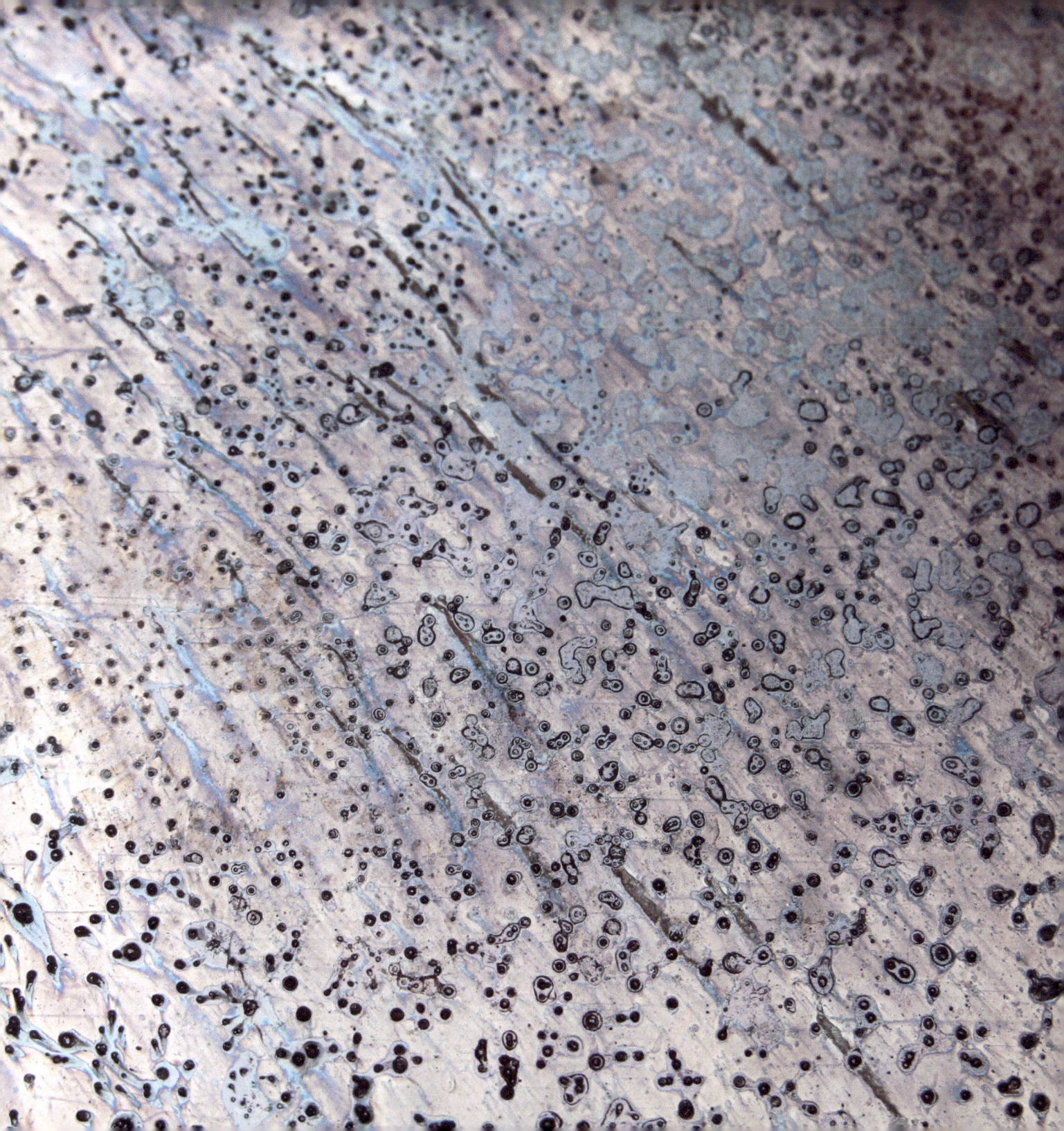

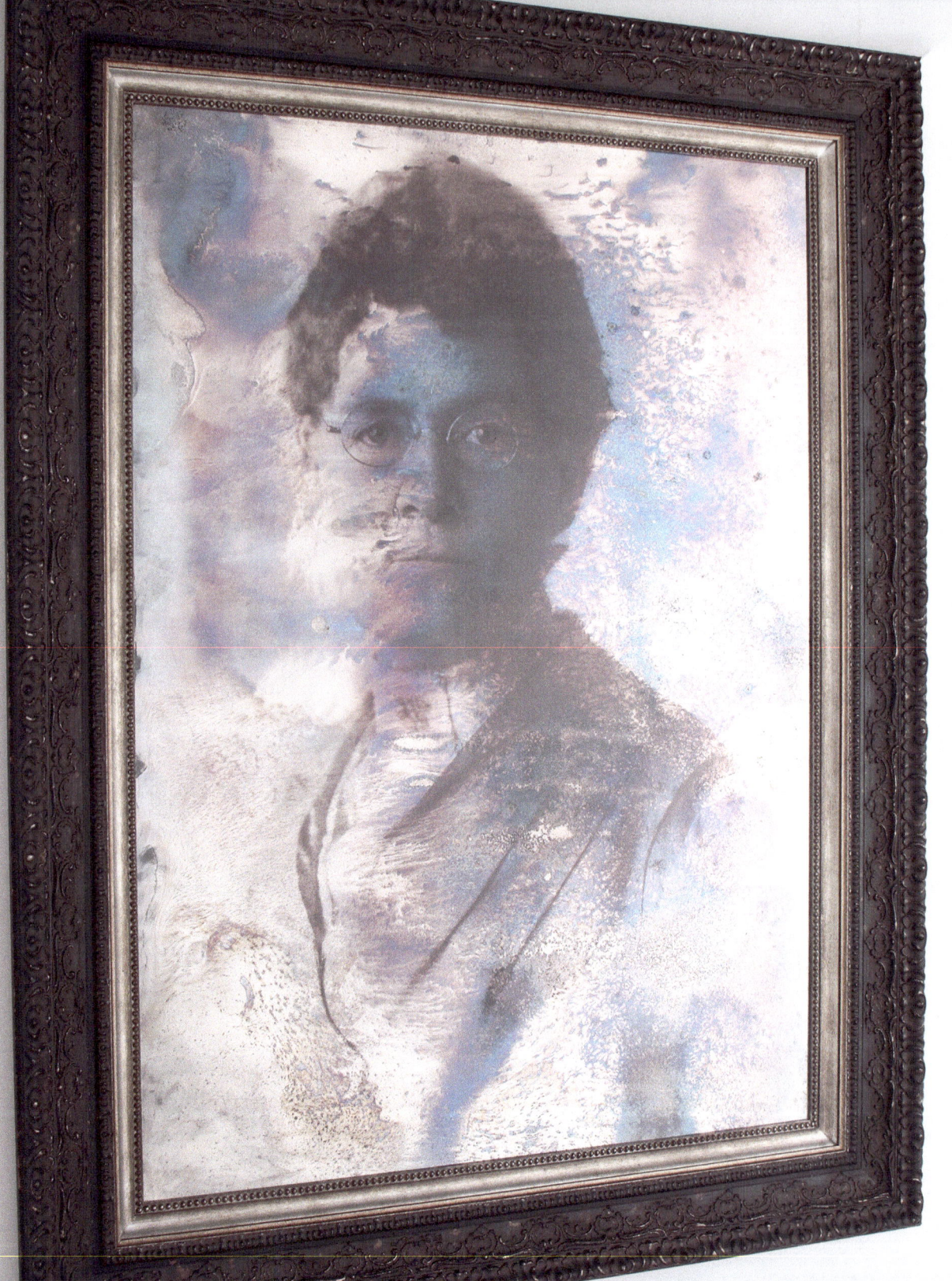

Martha Maria "Mattie" Hughes Cannon
(July 1, 1857 – July 10, 1932)

A polygamous wife, physician, Utah women's rights advocate and suffragist, and Utah State Senator, Marth Hughes Cannon was born in Wales and came to America with her family of Mormon converts.

At the age of sixteen she began her studies in science and eventually received her Bachelors degree in Chemistry from The University of Deseret (currently the University of Utah.) Her studies continued at the University of Michigan where she received her MD. At the age of 24, in 1881, she moved to Philadelphia to take post-graduate courses at the Auxiliary Medical Department of the University of Pennsylvania. Hughes was the only women out of 75 students. Additionally, Hughes took night classes to learn more about pharmaceuticals and enrolled at the National School of Elocution and Oratory. In 1882, she earned a Bachelors of Science from the University of Pennsylvania and a bachelor's degree in Oratory at the National School of Elocution and Oratory. At 25, Martha Hughes had earned four degrees.

She became the fourth of six wives in a polygamous marriage to Angus M. Cannon, a prominent Mormon leader during the anti-polygamy crusade. Cannon exiled herself to Europe so that she wouldn't have to testify against her husband. Upon returning to Utah, Cannon worked as a doctor and fought for women's rights. She helped put women enfranchisement into Utah's constitution when it was granted statehood in 1896. On November 3, 1896 Cannon became the first female State Senator elected in the United States. She defeated her own husband, who was also on the ballot. Martha Hughes Cannon was the author of Utah Sanitation Laws and was a founder and member of Utah's first State Board of Health.

Women's Suffrage in Utah

While the Mormons gained power by gathering in the Utah territory, their practice of plural marriage or polygamy, came under increased scrutiny by the Federal Government and women's rights advocates. Anti-polygamy activists came together within the Utah territory "to fight to the death that system which so enslaves and degrades our sex, and which robs them of so much happiness." Polygamy was a sensational topic through the United States and many were convinced that it would help end polygamy if Mormon women had the right to vote.

A New York suffragist, Hamilton Wilcox, proposed testing women suffrage in the territories in 1867, specifically in Utah because of the large population of females. He believed that as a "fringe benefit, the Mormon system of plural wives would be eliminated."

In 1869 Congress made a move to increase federal authority over Utah Territory and prevent polygamists from holding public office. Mormon women heavily protested the bill, rallying together in Salt Lake City to protest the legislation. During this time, the Utah Legislative Authority considered the enfranchisement of women in Utah territory. After two weeks by unanimous vote, the Utah Legislature passed a bill enfranchising women. To delegate William Henry Hooper the reason for enfranchisement was, "To convince the country how utterly without foundation the popular assertions were concerning the women of the Territory, some members of the Legislative Assembly were in favor of passing the law." Acting governor of Utah Territory, S. A. Mann, signed the law on February 12, 1870. Women above the age of twenty-one were now allowed to vote in Utah Territory, which was 50 years before it would be Federally mandated.

The Edmunds–Tucker Act of 1887, disincorporated both the LDS Church and the Perpetual Emigration Fund on the grounds that they fostered polygamy. The act prohibited the practice of polygamy and punished it with a fine of $500 to $800 and imprisonment of up to five years. It dissolved the corporation of the church and directed the confiscation by the federal government of all church properties valued over a limit of $50,000. The act was enforced by the U.S. Marshal and a host of deputies.

The Act also disenfranchised women in Utah, who would have to wait until the 19th Amendment to the Constitution was passed in 1920 to regain the right to vote.

In 1890 the U.S. Supreme Court upheld the seizure of Church property under the Edmunds–Tucker Act in *Late Corporation of the Church of Jesus Christ of Latter-Day Saints v. United States.*
This act was repealed in 1978.

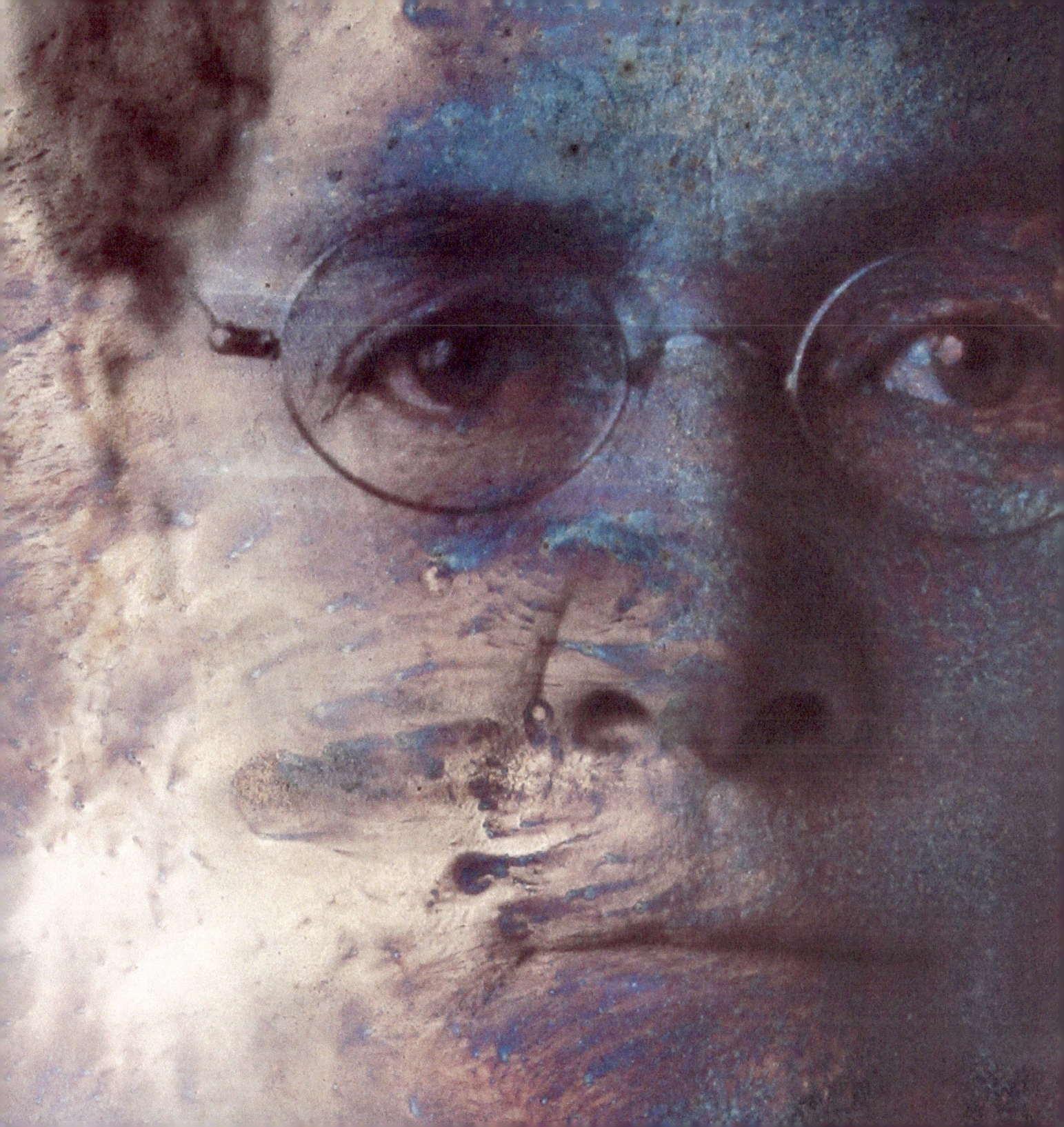

William Moses Kunstler
(July 7, 1919 – September 4, 1995)

An American radical lawyer and civil rights activist, William Kunstler was widely known for his politically unpopular clients. Kunstler's defense of the Chicago Seven from 1969–1970 led The New York Times to label him "the country's most controversial and, perhaps, its best-known lawyer." The trial, which had many aspects of guerrilla theater, was a well publicized demonstration of Kunstler "putting the system on trial."

His clients were often high profile individuals who were working to change institutional systems such as; Catonsville Nine, the Black Panther Party, the Weather Underground Organization, the Attica Prison rioters, the American Indian Movement and dozens of American soldiers who refused to fight and claimed conscientious objector status.

He also represented those who were already seen as guilty in the court of public opinion. Kunstler argued that there is a bias built into the system that makes it impossible for many individuals to receive a fair trial. Individuals such as: Jack Ruby, El-Sayyid Nosair, the assassin of the late Jewish leader Rabbi Meir Kahane, who was acquitted of murder charges. Assata Shakur in 1977, charged in New Jersey with a variety of felonies in connection with a 1973 shootout with New Jersey State Troopers. Sheikh Omar Abdel-Rahman, head of the Egyptian-based terrorist group Gama'a al-Islamiyah, responsible for the 1993 World Trade Center bombing. Colin Ferguson, the man responsible for the 1993 Long Island Rail Road shooting. Qubilah Shabazz, the daughter of Malcolm X, accused of plotting to murder Louis Farrakhan of the Nation of Islam. Glenn Harris, a New York City public school teacher who absconded with a fifteen-year-old girl for two months. Nico Minardos, a flamboyant actor indicted by Rudy Giuliani for conspiracy to ship arms to Iran. Darrell Cabey, one of the persons shot by Bernard Goetz, and associates of the Gambino crime family.

His techniques for defending his clients were often viewed as unusual. He focused on highlighting the culture that the case was operating within rather than accepting the traditional framework of the system.

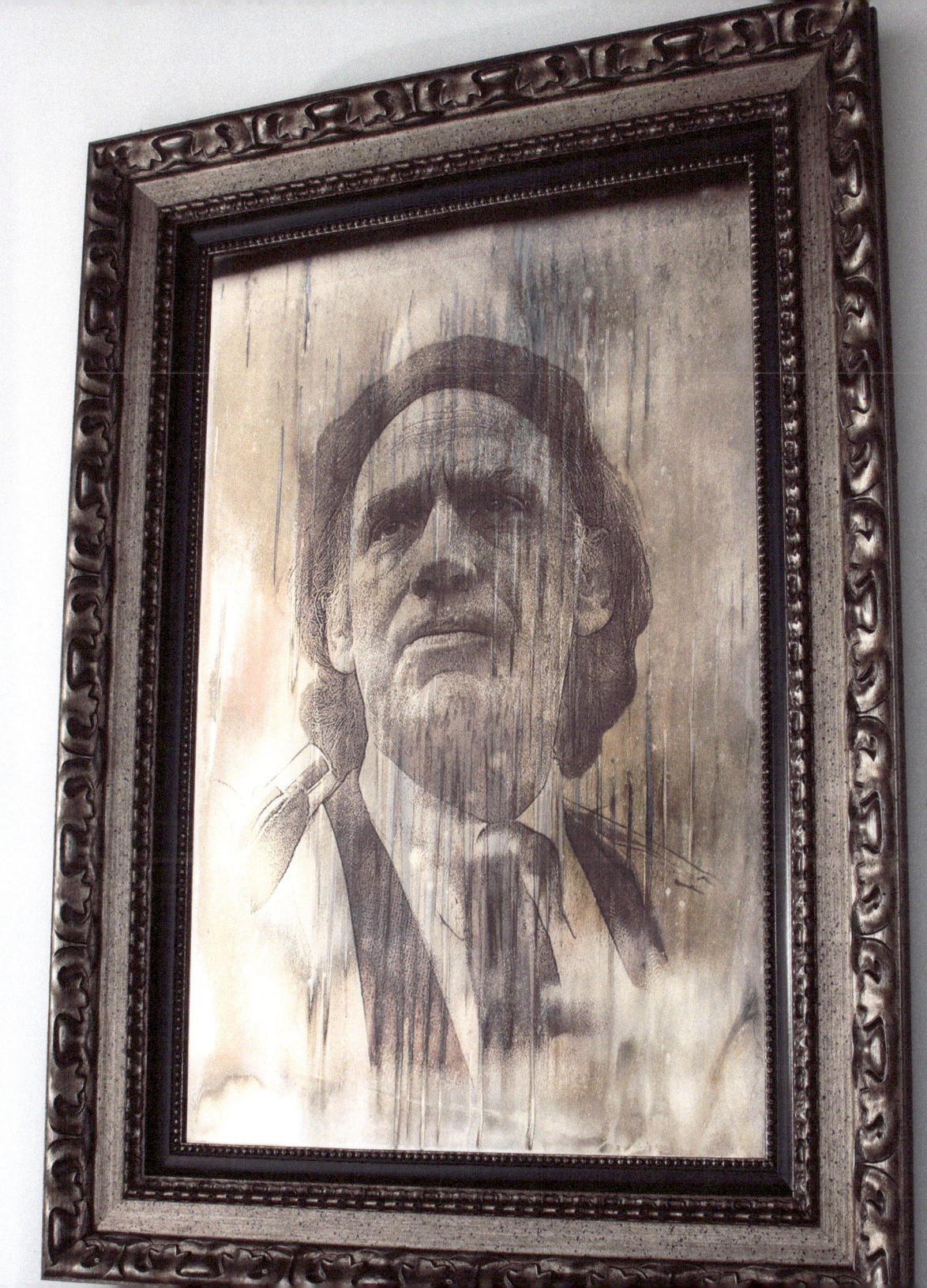

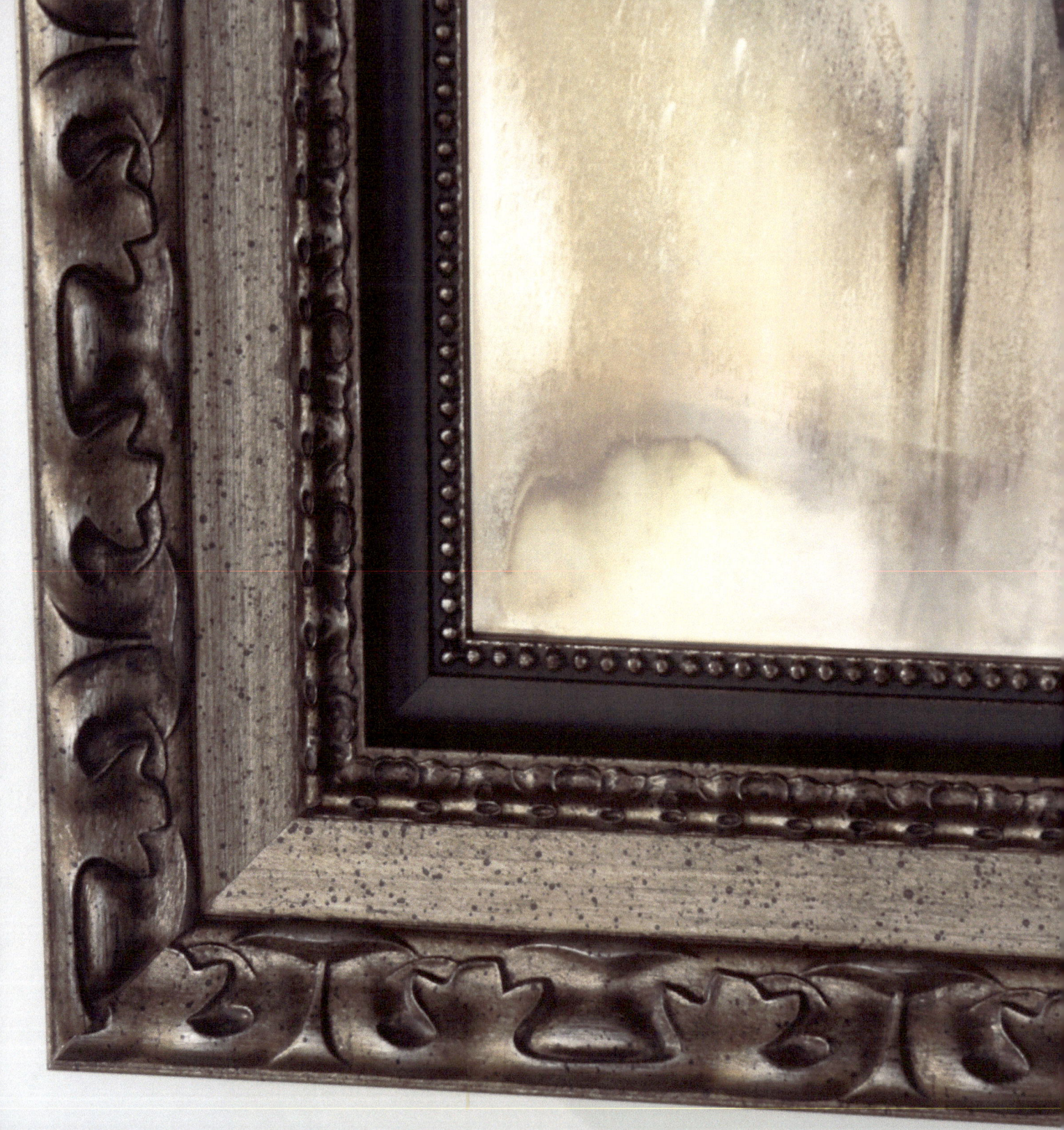

William Kunstler Quotes on Legality

"And that's the terrible myth of organized society. That everything that's done through the established system is legal. And that word has a powerful psychological impact. It makes people believe that there is an order to life and an order to a system. And that a person who goes through this order and is convicted has gotten all that is due him and therefore society can turn its conscious off and look to other things and other times. And that's the terrible thing about these past trials that they have this aura of legitimacy an aura of legality. I suspect that better men than the world has known and more of them have gone to their deaths through a legal system then through all the illegalities in the history of man. Six million people in Europe during the Third Reich, legal, Sacco and Vanzetti, quite legal, the Haymarket defendants, legal, the hundreds of rape trials throughout the south where black men were condemned to death all legal, Jesus legal, Socrates legal and that is the kaleidoscopic nature of what we live through here and in other places because all tyrants learn that it is far better to do this thing through some semblance of legality than to do it without that pretext."

"You can crucify a Jesus, you can poison a Socrates, you can hang John Brown or Nathan Hale, you can kill a Che Guevara, you can jail a Eugene Debs or a Bobby Seale. You can assassinate John Kennedy or a Martin Luther King, but the problems remain, the hangman's rope never solved a single problem except that of one man."

The Chicago Seven
(originally Chicago Eight, also Conspiracy Eight/Conspiracy Seven)

Seven defendants—Abbie Hoffman, Jerry Rubin, David Dellinger, Tom Hayden, Rennie Davis, John Froines, and Lee Weiner—were charged by the federal government with conspiracy, inciting to riot, and other charges related to anti-Vietnam War and countercultural protests that took place in Chicago, Illinois, on the occasion of the 1968 Democratic National Convention. Bobby Seale, the eighth man charged, had his trial severed during the proceedings. This lowered the number of defendants from eight to seven.

A significant element of this trial was Kuntsler's approach of putting the system on trail. This would become a central theme in his career. Rather than focusing on the guilt or innocence of the accused, he would use these trials as social commentary. He was forcing the judge and the public at large to consider their own preconceptions. In this case we can imagine that the trail was initially designed to decide if the defendants had acted lawfully in their actions. Kunstler asserted that perhaps the war was unlawful and that the actions taken by the protesters were within their rights. He shifted the focus of the trail away from the existing laws regarding protest to ask how the public might display disagreement with their government, when that same government writes the laws regarding protest.

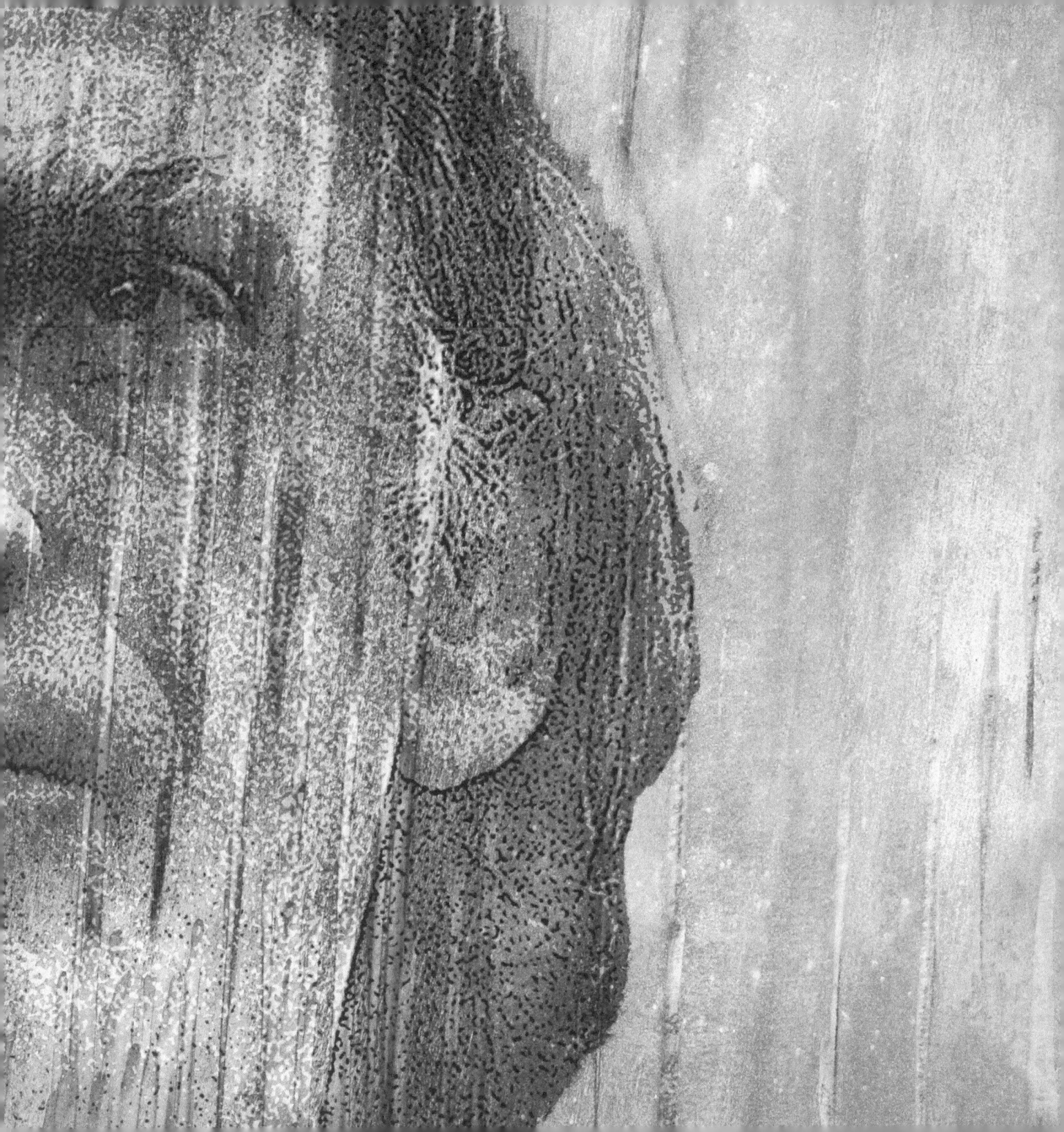

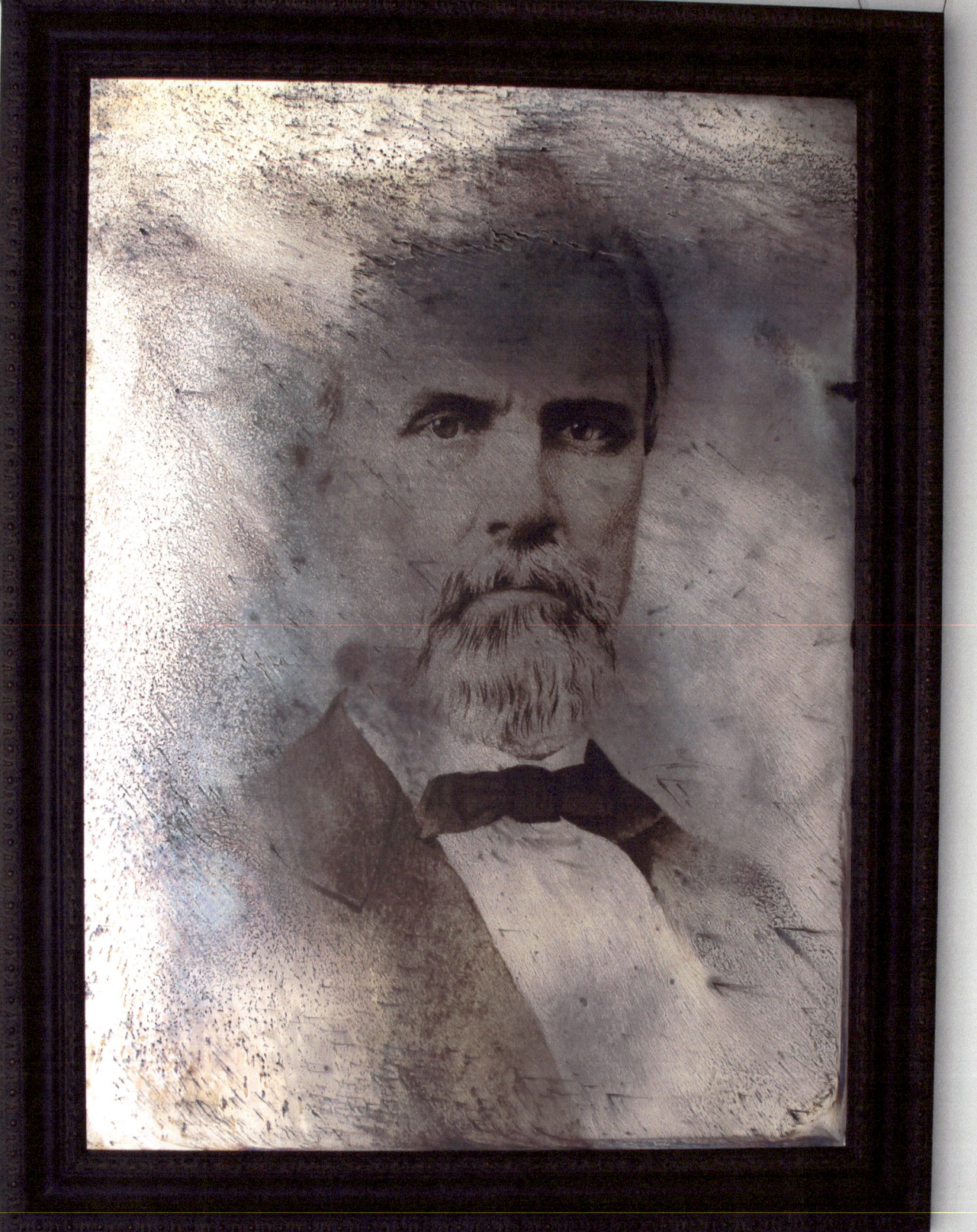

Nathan Bedford Forrest
(July 13, 1821 – October 29, 1877)

Nathan Bedford Forrest was very financially successful cotton farmer and slave trader.

Nicknamed "The Wizard of The Saddle" for his revolutionary use of horseback mounted soldiers in the cause of the Confederate States durning the American Civil War, Forrest was known as a brilliant tactician. He was one of the few officers on either side of the war to rise to the level of general after enlisting as a private. Union General Ulysses S. Grant proclaimed him as "the most remarkable man our civil war produced on either side."

At the end of the war, Forrest gave a remarkable farewell speech to his troops in which he called upon them to "divest" themselves of the feelings that the war had stirred up, namely "feelings of animosity, hatred, and revenge." (a partial transcript of this speech appears on the panel below.)

After the war, Forrest became one of the earliest members of the Ku Klux Klan (the KKK.) There is a belief that the term "Grand Wizard," which refers to the leader of the KKK, is derived from Forrests nickname. He is believed to be the first leader of that organization.

After only one year of this leadership he became disillusioned by the disorganization of the membership and the violence that the KKK was inflicting on the recently freed blacks. He issued KKK General Order Number One: "It is therefore ordered and decreed, that the masks and costumes of this order be entirely abolished and destroyed."

This obviously resulted in a split between Forrest and the KKK. He went on to speak out against acts of violence towards blacks and specifically offered his services to the Governor of Tennessee "to exterminate the white marauders who disgrace their race by this cowardly murder of Negroes."

Towards the end of his life he gave a speech on July 5, 1875 to the Independent Order of Pole-Bearers Association, an organization of black Southerners working to improve the economic condition of blacks and to gain equal rights for all Americans. (Speech transcript is presented on the panel below.)
This speech caused pro-white southern organizations to denounce Forrest.

In the 1994 film "Forrest Gump," the title character reveals that he was named after his fore-father General Nathan Bedford Forrest, pointing out that he "… started up this club called the Ku Klux Klan."

Speech before the Independent Order of Pole-Bearers Association

Ladies and Gentlemen I accept the flowers as a memento of reconciliation between the white and colored races of the southern states. I accept it more particularly as it comes from a colored lady, for if there is any one on God's earth who loves the ladies I believe it is myself. (Immense applause and laughter.) This day is a day that is proud to me, having occupied the position that I did for the past twelve years, and been misunderstood by your race. This is the first opportunity I have had during that time to say that I am your friend. I am here a representative of the southern people, one more slandered and maligned than any man in the nation.

I will say to you and to the colored race that men who bore arms and followed the flag of the Confederacy are, with very few exceptions, your friends. I have an opportunity of saying what I have always felt – that I am your friend, for my interests are your interests, and your interests are my interests. We were born on the same soil, breathe the same air, and live in the same land. Why, then, can we not live as brothers? I will say that when the war broke out I felt it my duty to stand by my people. When the time came I did the best I could, and I don't believe I flickered. I came here with the jeers of some white people, who think that I am doing wrong. I believe that I can exert some influence, and do much to assist the people in strengthening fraternal relations, and shall do all in my power to bring about peace. It has always been my motto to elevate every man- to depress none. (Applause.) I want to elevate you to take positions in law offices, in stores, on farms, and wherever you are capable of going.

I have not said anything about politics today. I don't propose to say anything about politics. You have a right to elect whom you please; vote for the man you think best, and I think, when that is done, that you and I are freemen. Do as you consider right and honest in electing men for office. I did not come here to make you a long speech, although invited to do so by you. I am not much of a speaker, and my business prevented me from preparing myself. I came to meet you as friends, and welcome you to the white people. I want you to come nearer to us. When I can serve you I will do so. We have but one flag, one country; let us stand together. We may differ in color, but not in sentiment. Use your best judgment in selecting men for office and vote as you think right.

Many things have been said about me which are wrong, and which white and black persons here, who stood by me through the war, can contradict. I have been in the heat of battle when colored men, asked me to protect them. I have placed myself between them and the bullets of my men, and told them they should be kept unharmed. Go to work, be industrious, live honestly and act truly, and when you are oppressed I'll come to your relief. I thank you, ladies and gentlemen, for this opportunity you have afforded me to be with you, and to assure you that I am with you in heart and in hand" (Prolonged applause.)

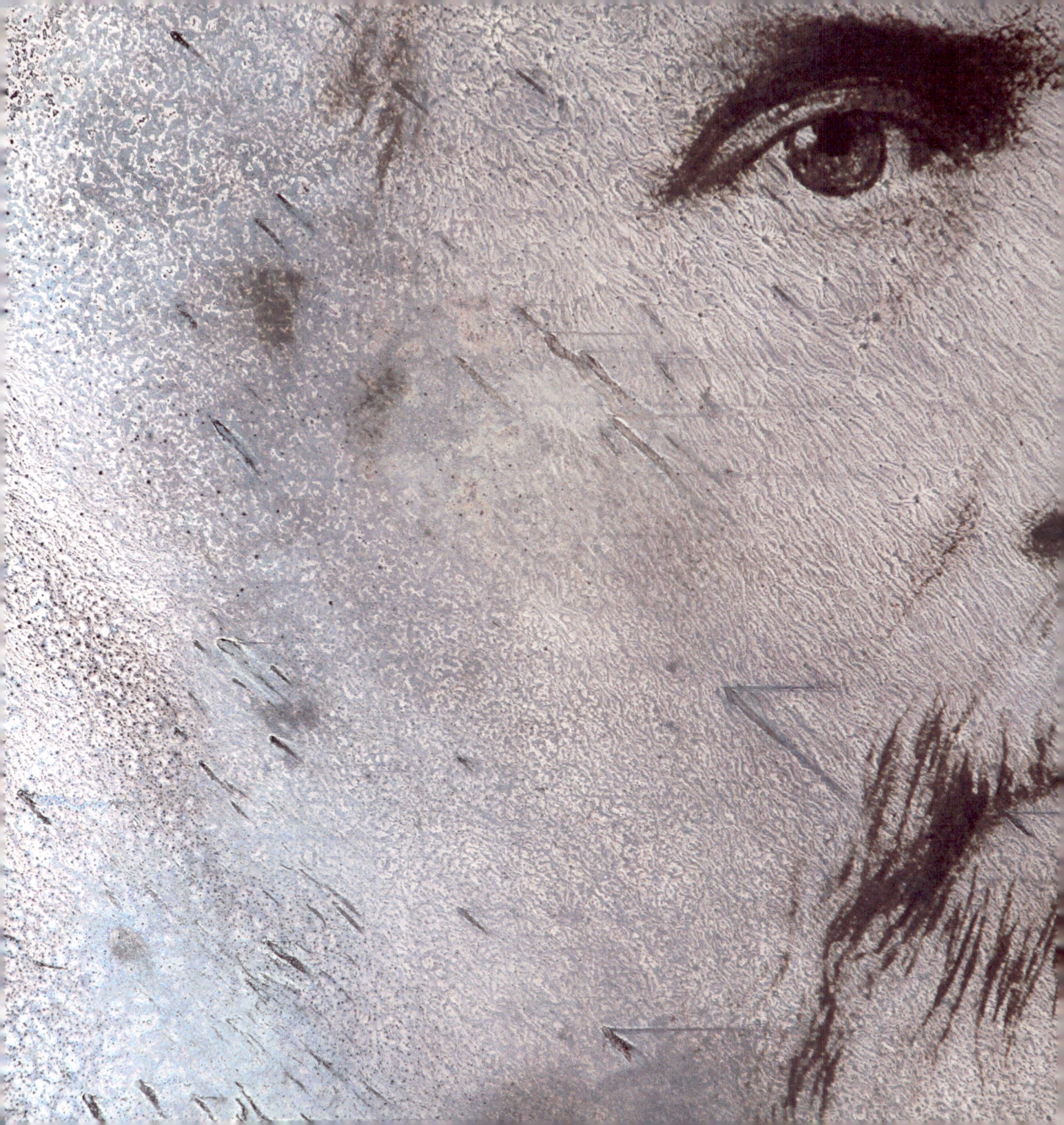

The following text is excerpted from Forrest's farewell address to his troops:

Civil war, such as you have just passed through naturally engenders feelings of animosity, hatred, and revenge. It is our duty to divest ourselves of all such feelings; and as far as it is in our power to do so, to cultivate friendly feelings towards those with whom we have so long contended, and heretofore so widely, but honestly, differed. Neighborhood feuds, personal animosities, and private differences should be blotted out; and, when you return home, a manly, straightforward course of conduct will secure the respect of your enemies. Whatever your responsibilities may be to Government, to society, or to individuals meet them like men.

The attempt made to establish a separate and independent Confederation has failed; but the consciousness of having done your duty faithfully, and to the end, will, in some measure, repay for the hardships you have undergone. In bidding you farewell, rest assured that you carry with you my best wishes for your future welfare and happiness. Without, in any way, referring to the merits of the Cause in which we have been engaged, your courage and determination, as exhibited on many hard-fought fields, has elicited the respect and admiration of friend and foe. And I now cheerfully and gratefully acknowledge my indebtedness to the officers and men of my command whose zeal, fidelity and unflinching bravery have been the great source of my past success in arms.

I have never, on the field of battle, sent you where I was unwilling to go myself; nor would I now advise you to a course which I felt myself unwilling to pursue. You have been good soldiers, you can be good citizens. Obey the laws, preserve your honor, and the Government to which you have surrendered can afford to be, and will be, magnanimous.

—N.B. Forrest, Lieut.-General
Headquarters, Forrest's Cavalry Corps
Gainesville, Alabama
May 9, 1865.

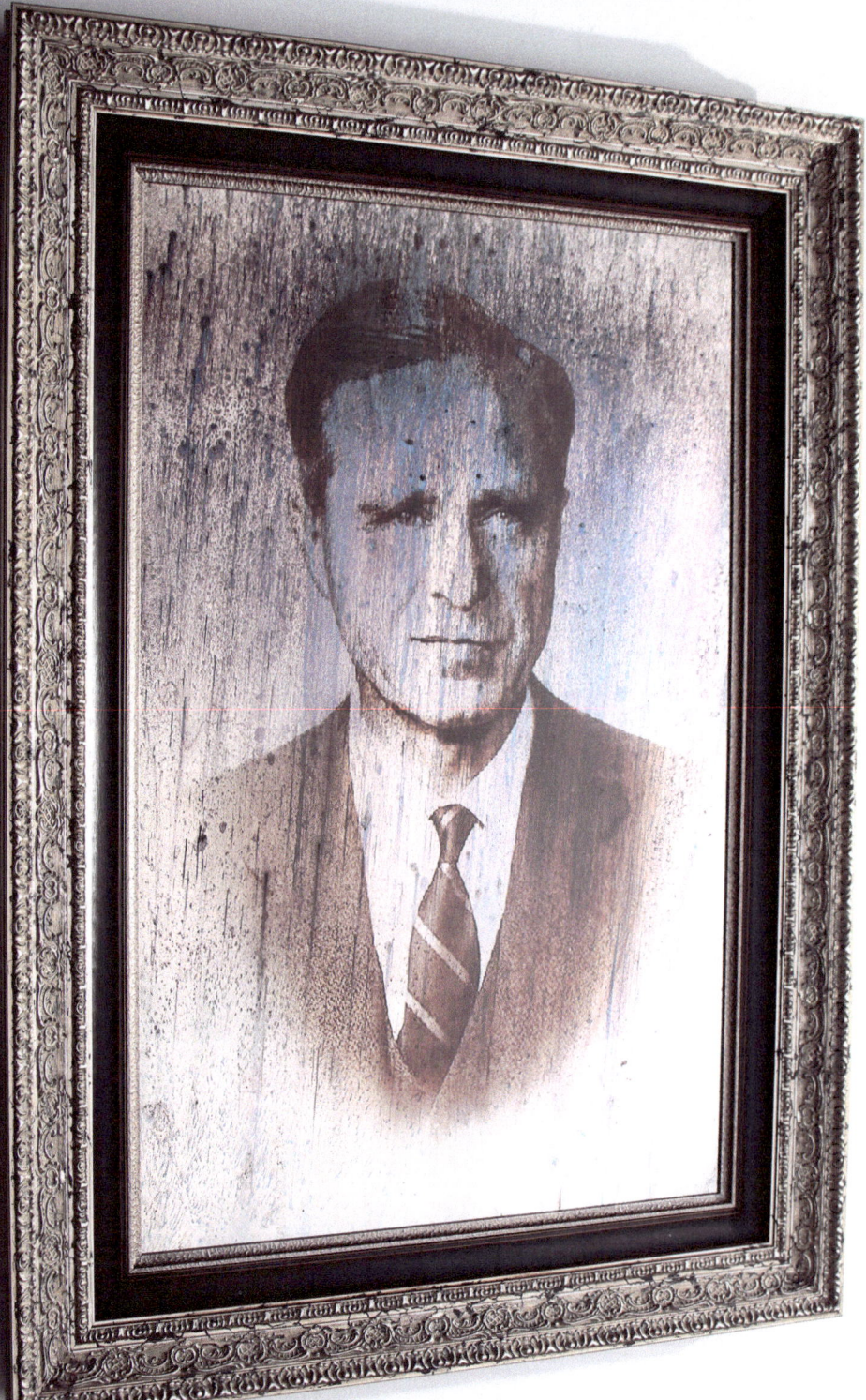

Prescott Sheldon Bush Sr.
(May 15, 1895 – October 8, 1972)

An American banker and politician, Prescott Bush was the father of President George H. W. Bush. He is the grandfather of President George W. Bush and Governor Jeb Bush.

A former student at Yale College, Prescott Bush was admitted to the Zeta Psi Fraternity and The Skull and Bones Secret Society. George H. W. Bush and George W. Bush were also members of this society. According to Skull and Bones lore, Prescott Bush was among a group of Bonesmen who dug up and removed the skull of Geronimo from his grave at Fort Sill, Oklahoma, in 1918. According to historian David L. Miller, the Bonesmen probably dug up somebody at Fort Sill, but not Geronimo.

After graduation, Bush served as a Field Artillery Captain with the American Expeditionary Forces (1917–1919) during World War I. He received intelligence training at Verdun, France and was briefly assigned to a staff of French officers. Alternating between intelligence and artillery, he came under fire in the Meuse-Argonne offensive.

Bush was the founder and one of seven directors of the Union Banking Corporation (holding a single share out of 4,000), an investment bank that operated as a clearing house for many assets and enterprises held by German steel magnate Fritz Thyssen. In July 1942, the bank was suspected of holding gold on behalf of Nazi leaders. A subsequent government investigation disproved those allegations but confirmed the Thyssens' control. In October 1942 the United States seized the bank under the Trading with the Enemy Act which held the assets for the duration of World War II. Prescott Bush worked closely with Thyssen, who was a prominent Nazi financier, and continued to manage his accounts during the Nazi occupation.

He was also a leading financier for the Nixon campaign. It was through this connection to the White House that the Bush legacy of politics was born.

Prescott Bush was politically active on social issues. He was involved with the American Birth Control League as early as 1942 and served as the treasurer of the first National Capital Campaign of Planned Parenthood in 1947. He was also an early supporter of the United Negro College Fund, serving as chairman of the Connecticut branch in 1951.

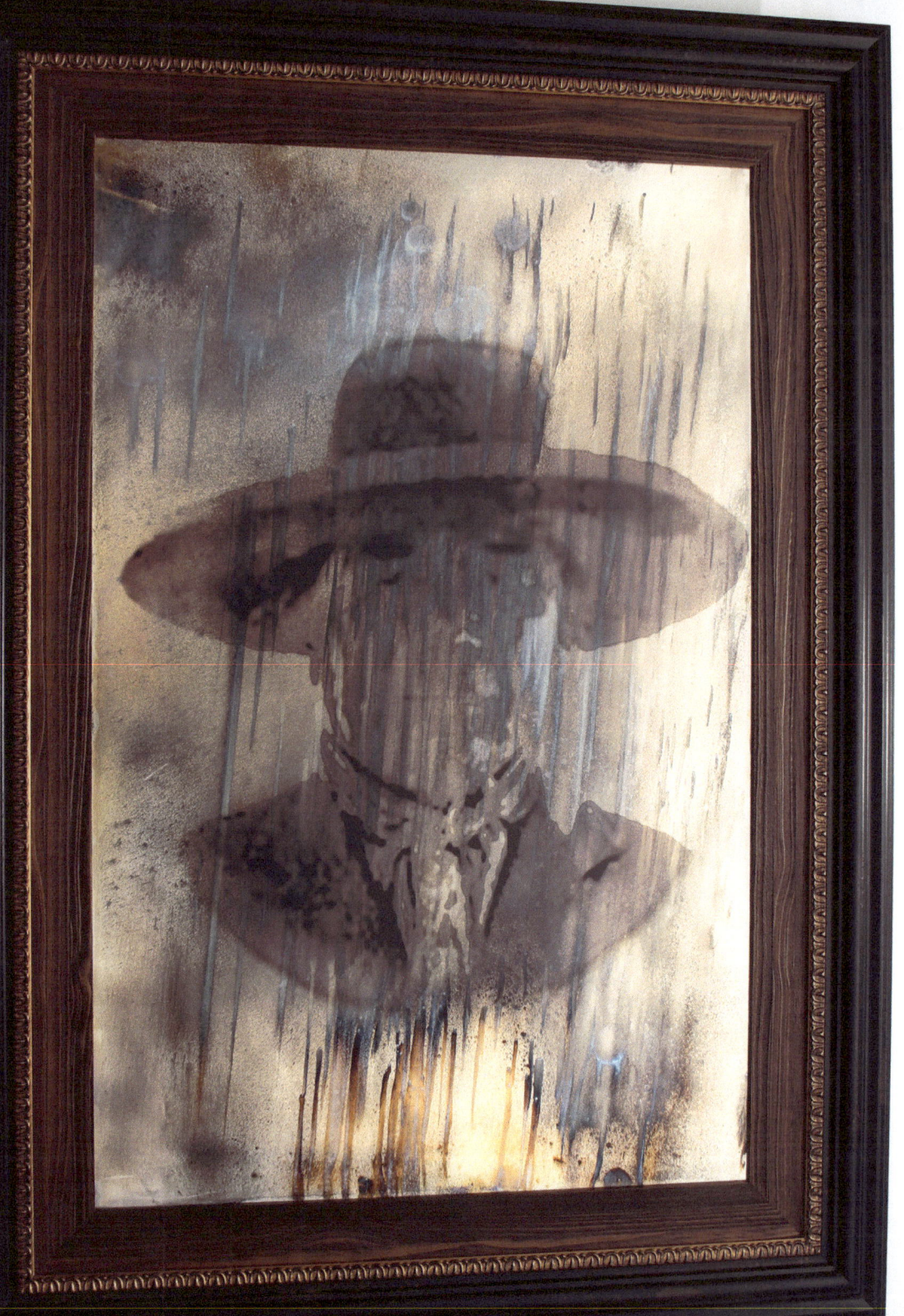

Wovoka also known as Jack Wilson
The Ghost Dance and Wounded Knee
(c. 1856 - September 20, 1932)

Jack Wilson, the prophet otherwise known as Wovoka, was believed to have had a vision during a solar eclipse on January 1, 1889. At the heart of this vision was a new dance, which would eventually become known as "The Ghost Dance." His belief was that if every Indian in the West danced The Ghost Dance all evil in the world would be swept away, leaving a renewed earth filled with food, love, and faith. Wovoka's preachings included messages of non-violence. Some native leaders allegedly emphasized the possible elimination of whites. This contributed to the existing defensive attitude of the federal officials, who were already fearful of the unfamiliar Ghost Dance movement.

In February 1890, the United States government broke a Lakota Treaty by adjusting the Great Sioux Reservation of South Dakota and breaking it up into smaller reservations to accommodate white homesteaders from the Eastern United States. In addition, it intended to "break up tribal relationships" and "conform Indians to the white man's ways, peaceably if they will, or forcibly if they must".

The Lakota were expected to farm and raise livestock and to send their children to boarding schools. The schools taught English, Christianity and American cultural practices with the goal of assimilation. They generally forbade inclusion of Indian traditional culture and language. The Ghost Dance and its prophecy stood in opposition to the government attempts to break up relationships between tribes and to prevent forms of traditional worship.

To help support the Lakota during the period of transition, the Bureau of Indian Affairs (BIA) was to supplement the Lakota with food and to hire white farmers as teachers for the people. The farming plan failed to take into account the difficulty that Lakota farmers would have in trying to cultivate crops in the semi-arid region of South Dakota. By the end of the 1890 growing season, a time of intense heat and low rainfall, it was clear that the land was unable to produce substantial agricultural yields. Unfortunately, this was also the time when the government's patience with supporting the so-called "lazy Indians" ran out. They cut rations for the Lakota in half. With the bison having been virtually eradicated a few years earlier, the Lakota were at risk of starvation.

December 29, 1890 - Spotted Elk was a Miniconjou leader on the U.S. Army's list of 'trouble-making' Indians. He was stopped while en route to convene with the remaining Lakota chiefs. U.S. Army officers forced him to relocate with his people to a small camp close to the Pine Ridge Agency. The soldiers could more closely watch the old chief at this location. That evening, December 28, the small band of Lakota erected their tipis on the banks of Wounded Knee Creek. The following day, during an attempt by the officers to collect weapons from the band, a young, deaf Lakota warrior refused to relinquish his arms. A struggle followed in which a weapon was discharged into the air. A U.S. officer gave the command to open fire and the Lakota responded by taking up previously confiscated weapons. The U.S. forces responded with carbine firearms and several rapid-fire light-artillery (Hotchkiss) guns mounted on the overlooking hill. When the fighting had concluded, 25 U.S. soldiers lay dead, many killed by friendly fire. Among the 153 dead Lakota, most were women and children.

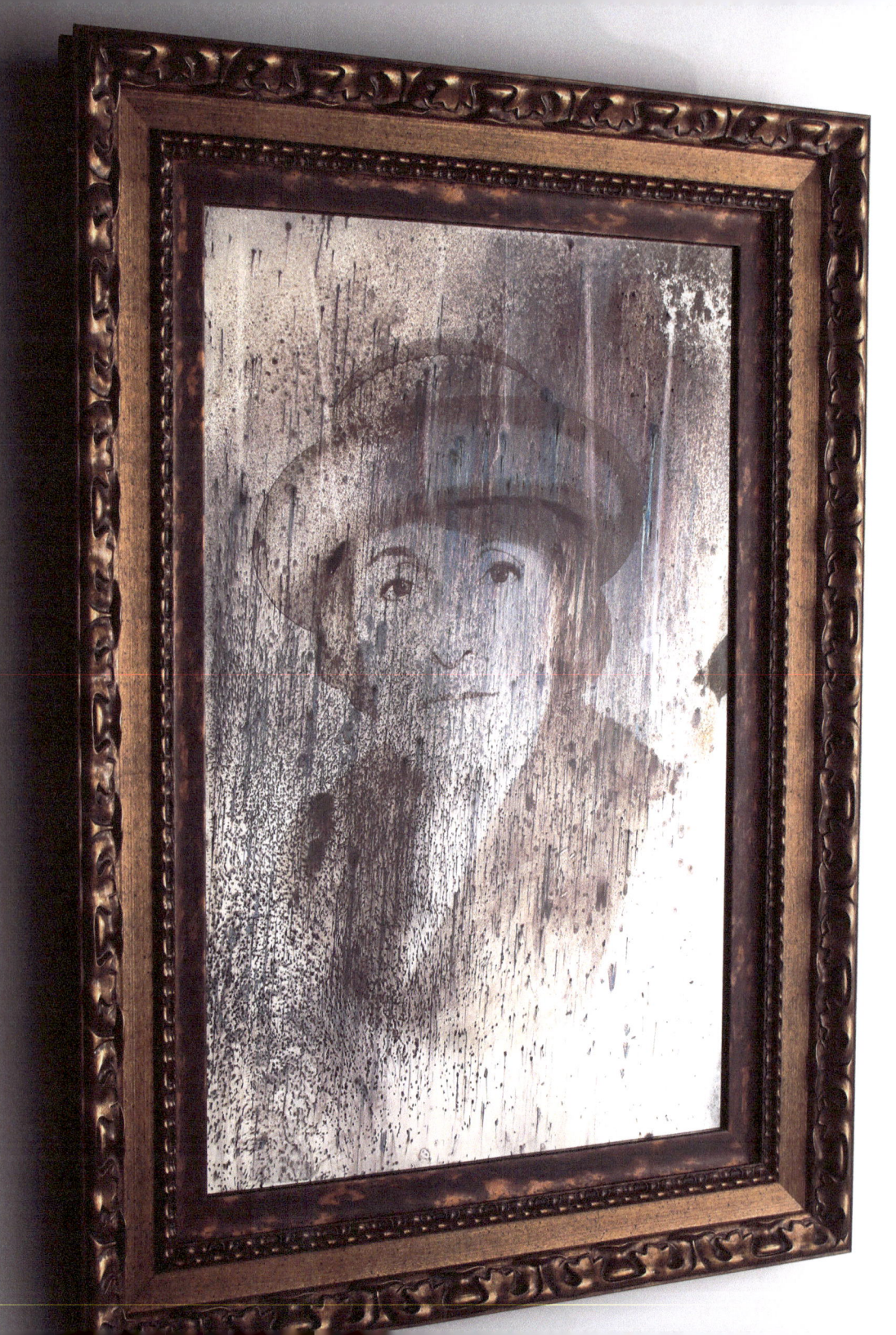

Margaret Higgins Sanger
born Margaret Louise Higgins,
also known as Margaret Sanger Slee
(September 14, 1879 – September 6, 1966)

An American birth control activist, sex educator, writer, and nurse, Margret Sanger popularized the term "birth control." She opened the first birth control clinic in the United States. In 1921 Sanger founded the American Birth Control League, which later became the Planned Parenthood Federation of America.

Due to her connection with Planned Parenthood, Sanger is a frequent target of criticism by opponents of abortion. However, Sanger drew a sharp distinction between birth control and abortion and was opposed to abortion through the bulk of her career. She believed that abortion was primarily a societal ill and public health danger that would disappear if women were able to prevent unwanted pregnancy.

In August 1914 Margaret Sanger was indicted for violating postal obscenity laws by sending The Woman Rebel through the postal system. This 16-page pamphlet contained detailed and precise information and graphic descriptions of various contraceptive methods. She fled the country rather than stand trial.

She was exposed to more open discussions of birth control in Europe then returned to America and founded The American Birth Control League (ABCL) in 1921. She enlarged her base of supporters by including the middle class. The founding principles of the ABCL were as follows:

We hold that children should be;
(1) Conceived in love,
(2) Born of the mother's conscious desire,
(3) and only begotten under conditions which render possible the heritage of health. Therefore, we hold that every woman must possess the power and freedom to prevent conception except when these conditions can be satisfied.

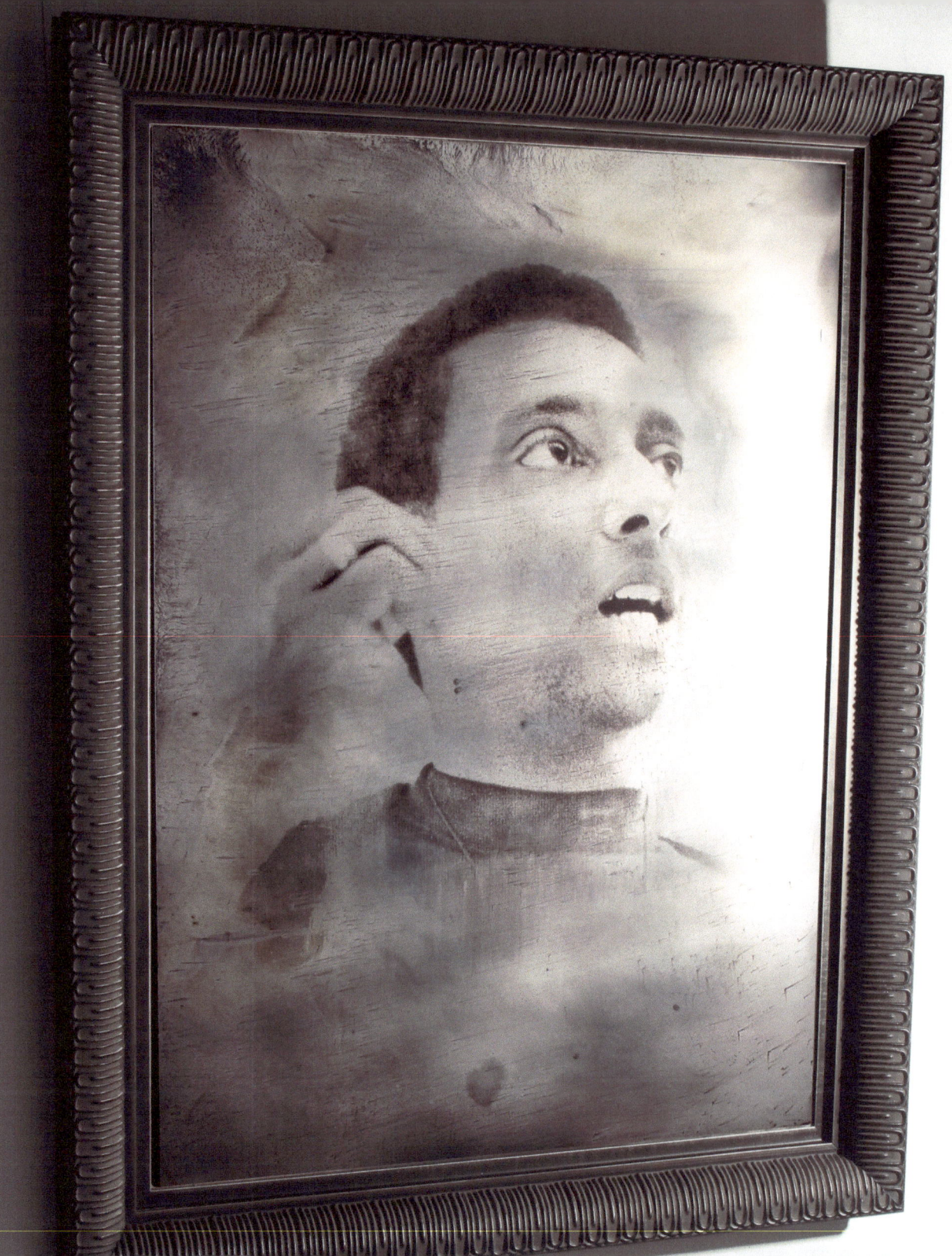

Kwame Ture (born Stokely Carmichael)
(June 29, 1941 – November 15, 1998)

A prominent organizer in the Civil Rights Movement in the United States and the global Pan-African movement, Stokely Carmichael was born in Trinidad. He grew up in the United States from the age of 11 and became an activist while attending Howard University. There he was the leader of the Student Nonviolent Coordinating Committee (SNCC.)

In 1964, Carmichael was project director for Mississippi's second congressional District. It was largely made up of the counties of the Mississippi Delta. Most blacks in Mississippi had been disenfranchised since the passage of a new state constitution in 1890. A summer project was to prepare them to register to vote and to conduct a parallel registration movement to demonstrate how much people wanted to vote. Grassroots activists organized the Mississippi Freedom Democratic Party (MFDP), because the regular Democratic Party did not represent African Americans in the state. At the end of this "Freedom Summer" In 1964, Carmichael went to the Democratic Convention in support of the MFDP, which sought to have its delegation seated. Although, the MFDP delegates were refused their voting rights by the Democratic National Committee. The Committee chose to seat the regular, white Jim Crow delegation. Carmichael, along with many SNCC staff members, left the convention with a profound sense of disillusionment in the American political system, which he later called "totalitarian liberal opinion."

Carmichael found the period of Selma to Montgomery Marches less and less effective after watching his protesters being brutally beaten once again. His disillusionment with the political system and his growing frustration with being drawn into non-violent encounters with police led him to collapse from the stress. While he continued his political work, his focus began to shift away from non-violent protest to a new notion of Black Power. He became the Honorary Prime Minister in the Black Panther Party.

Carmichael was one of the most popular and controversial radical African-American leaders of the late 1960s. J. Edgar Hoover, director of the FBI, secretly identified Carmichael as the man most likely to succeed Malcolm X as America's "black messiah." The FBI targeted him for personal destruction through its COINTELPRO program and Carmichael fled to Africa in 1968. He re-established himself in Ghana, then in Guinea, adopting the new name of Kwame Ture.

Kwame Ture, along with Charles V. Hamilton, is credited with coining the phrase "institutional racism"---defined as racism that occurs through institutions such as public bodies and corporations, including universities. In the late 1960s Ture defined "institutional racism" as "the collective failure of an organization to provide an appropriate and professional service to people because of their color, culture or ethnic origin."

Is it it easier to apply this idea of compassion for complexity when the subject is more distant?

Is it more challenging to hold this same complexity in those who are in our day to day thoughts?

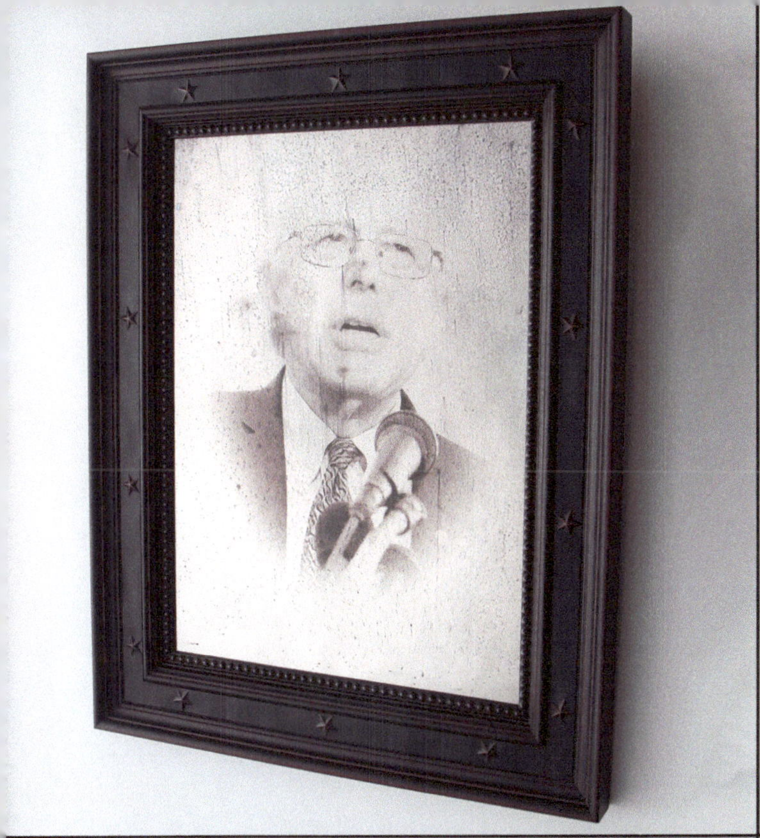

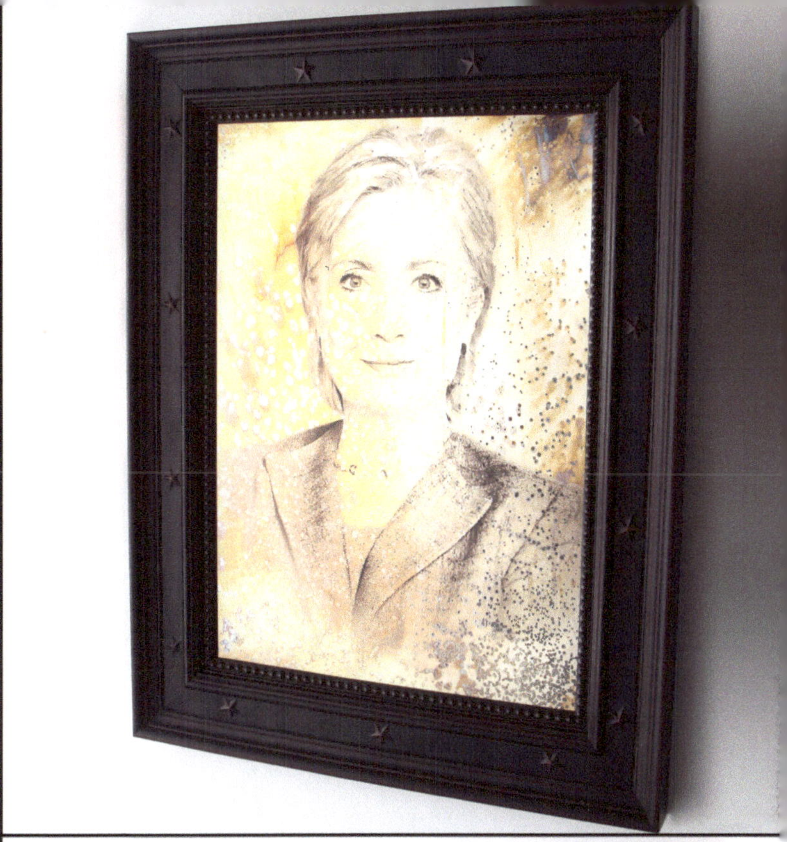

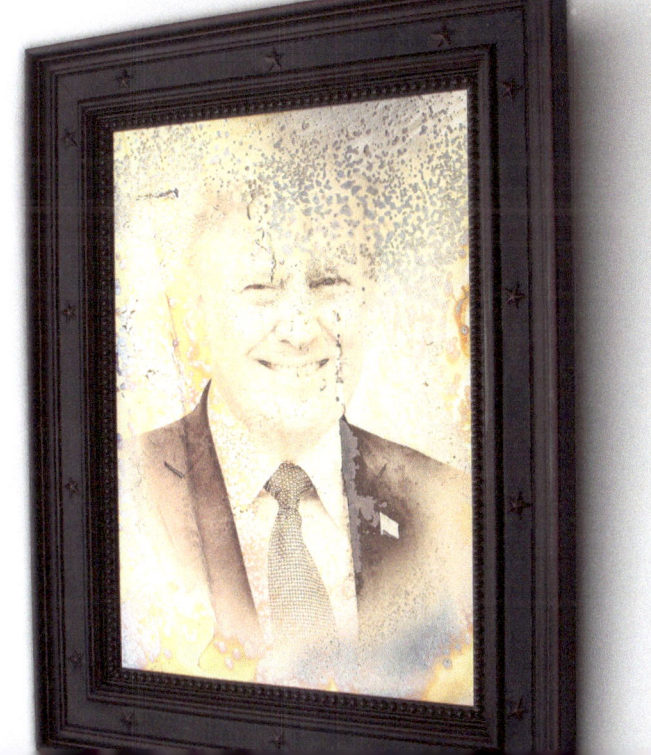
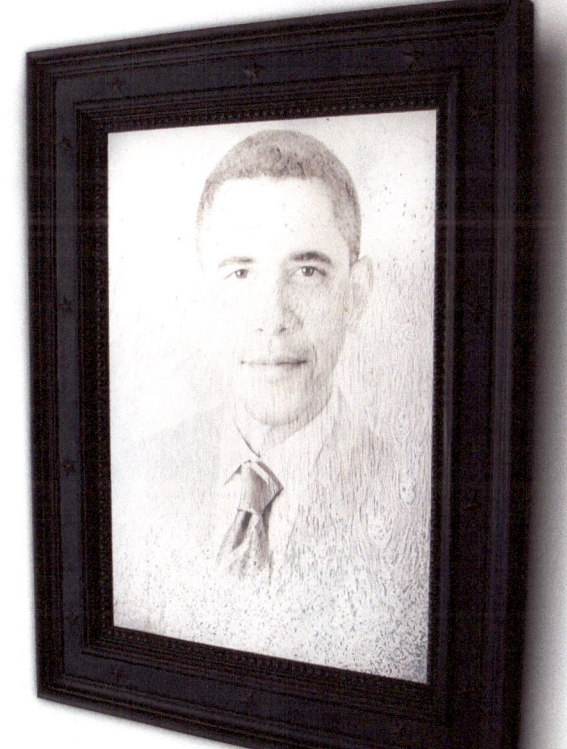

Scott Froschauer is an experimental artist who lives and works in Los Angeles, and he likes it there. His background consists of a structured education in Engineering, Theoretical Linguistics, Science, Art, Computer Programming and Business along with practical experience in Fabrication, Design, Non-ordinary Reality, Experiential Narrative, Venture Capital, Counterfeiting and Breathing.

Scott's work is first and foremost an exploration in emotional connectedness and empathy. He sees this as a political act and believes that our culture considers being connected to oneself as a revolutionary act. He attempts to create work that might expose and counteract the constant tides of alienation, judgement and addiction which our culture uses to avoid uncomfortable mental and emotional spaces.

It will all be ok in the end… so if it's not ok now, it's not over yet.

www.ingramcontent.com/pod-product-compliance
Lightning Source LLC
Chambersburg PA
CBHW040453220526
45473CB00004B/1624